To the Lord of Heaven
and Earth, for all He
has done and will do in and
through our lives.

For all those who are
willing to worship the Lord
in Spirit and Truth.

Lord, I Worship You...

LORD, I WORSHIP YOU...
Devotional Poem by Kathleen Schubitz

This poem is available in different size poster forms. Contact author for more information, kathy@RPJandco.com.

Published by:
RPJ & COMPANY, INC.
www.RPJandco.com
Orlando, Florida, U.S.A.

Scripture references are from the King James Version of the Bible. All rights reserved.

ISBN-13: 978-1-937770-38-9

Cover and Interior Design: Kathleen Schubitz

Cover Image: Meu mundo 214 © Sweet Angel - Fotolia.com

Printed in the United States of America.

Lord, I Worship You...

KATHLEEN SCHUBITZ

Lord, I worship You...
for Who You are,
For being close
and never far.

Genesis 15:1, Isaiah 12:2, Hebrews 13:5

Lord, I worship You...
for what You did
upon the Cross,
For how You came
to save the lost.

Matthew 18:11, Hebrews 12:2

Lord, I worship You...
for allowing the
Comforter in me to abide,
For revealing all truth
hidden deep down inside.

John 14:16, 16:13

Lord, I worship You...
for satisfying
my longing soul,
For transforming me
and making me whole.

Psalm 63:5, 107:9, Romans 12:2

Lord, I worship You...
for giving me breath,
For delivering my
soul from death.

Job 33:4, Psalm 18:4

Lord, I worship You...
for redeeming me
with Your blood,
For wrapping me in
Your light and love.

Romans 5:9, Psalm 119:105, Isaiah 60:19

Lord, I worship You...
for meeting my every need,
For providing me
with Kingdom seed.

Philippians 4:19, Malachi 3:10

Lord I worship You...
for restoring years
the locust has eaten,
For planting my feet
on a solid foundation.

Joel 2:25, Luke 6:48

Lord, I worship You...
for being my very best friend,
For staying with
me until the end.

Proverbs 18:24, Matthew 10:22, Matthew 24:13

Lord, I worship You...
for creating me to follow You,
For revealing Your
heart and making me new.

Daniel 2:30, Matthew 16:24, John 10:27

Lord, I worship You...
for filling me with power,
For being my
strength and high tower.

Romans 15:13, Psalm 18:2

Lord, I worship You...
for ruling and reigning
in authority,
For upholding me
with integrity.

Isaiah 32:1, Psalm 41:12

Lord, I worship You...
for the anointing in me,
For breaking heavy yokes
to set captives free.

1 John 2:27, Matthew 11:29-30

Lord, I worship You...
for being my
husband and counselor,
For being my
Everlasting Father.

Isaiah 9:6, 54:5

Lord, I worship You...
for lifting me higher,
For fulfilling my heart's desire.

Matthew 9:13, Psalm 21:2, 37:4

Lord, I worship You...
for rebuking the devourer
for my sake,
For instructing and teaching
me without mistake.

Malachi 3:11, Psalm 32:8

Lord, I worship You...
for ordering each
and every step,
For bringing good
from all my mess.

Psalm 37:23, Romans 8:28

Lord, I worship You...
for supplying clothing,
shelter and food,
For providing all things,
they are good.

Matthew 6:25, Proverbs 28:10, Matthew 7:11

Lord, I worship You...
for working
behind the scenes,
For making me
victorious over enemies.

Matthew 6:8, 1 Corinthians 15:57

Lord, I worship You...
for being my partner
and co-laborer,
For monitoring my every
thought and behavior.

Philemon 1:17, 1 Timothy 3:2, Titus 2:3

Lord, I worship You...
for holding me close
so I won't stumble,
For being my ever-present
help in trouble.

Proverbs 3:23, Psalm 46:1

Lord, I worship You...
for lifting my head
above my enemies,
For commanding Your
lovingkindness toward me.

Psalm 27:6, 42:8

Lord, I worship You...
for protecting me and
keeping me safe,
For helping me finish
running the race.

Psalm 91:2, Hebrews 12:1

Lord, I worship You...
for renewing my youth
with eagle-like wings,
For satisfying my mouth
with good things.

Psalm 103:5

Lord, I worship You...
for upholding me with
Your hand of righteousness,
For filling my hungry soul
with Your goodness.

Isaiah 41:10, Psalm 107:9

Lord, I worship You...
for speaking truth to
the inward parts of me,
For completing the good
work You've begun in me.

Psalm 51:6, Philippians 1:6

Lord, I worship You...
for teaching me
all Your ways,
For always guiding,
never leading me astray.

Psalm 27:11, 119:67, Proverbs 7:25

Lord, I worship You...
for being my High Priest,
For filling me with a love
that will never cease.

Hebrews 2:17, 1 John 3:1

Lord, I worship You...
for sitting me at the
Father's right hand,
For washing me with the
Blood of the Lamb.

Psalm 110:1, Revelation 1:5

Lord, I worship You...
for being my
Lord of Lords,
For being with me
now and forevermore.

Psalm 136:3

Lord, I worship You...
for ordering my steps
and giving purpose to life,
For helping me live
daily without strife.

Psalm 119:133, Proverbs 15:18

Lord, I worship You...
for establishing me and
keeping me from evil,
For filling my soul as
I read the Bible.

2 Thessalonians 3:3, Psalm 107:9

Lord, I worship You...
for being my
King of Kings,
For touching my heart
and making me sing.

2 Thessalonians 3:3, Psalm 107:9

Lord, I worship You...
for giving me love
for my enemies,
For removing opposition
so Jesus comes forth in me.

Matthew 5:44, Galatians 4:6

Lord, I worship You...
for Your Holy Spirit
living within,
For cleansing me deeply
and forgiving all my sin.

1 John 1:9, Psalm 51:2

Lord, I worship You...
for creating me
to walk in health,
For giving me access
to Kingdom wealth.

Proverbs 4:22, 10:22, 13:22

Lord, I worship You...
for being my
strength and shield,
For lifting me
when I'm on my knees.

Psalm 28:7, Ephesians 3:14

Lord, I worship You...
for treading down my enemies,
For healing me of every disease.

Psalm 108:13, Matthew 9:35, Luke 4:40

Lord, I worship You...
for girding me
with gladness,
For touching my heart
and removing all sadness.

Psalm 30:11, Ecclesiastes 7:3

Lord, I worship You...
for filling my
basket and my cup,
For encouraging me
to always look up.

Malachi 3:10, Psalm 5:3

Lord, I worship You...
for pouring out
Your spirit upon me,
For revealing Your
glory in me and through me.

Isaiah 61:1, 1 Peter 4:13, 5:1

Lord, I worship You...
for filling my heart with praise,
For giving me spiritual eyes
to see through the haze.

Psalm 111:1, Ezekiel 40:4

Lord, I worship You...
for giving me wisdom
when I ask,
For clearly leading me
in a plain path.

James 1:5, Proverbs 3:6, Psalm 27:11

Lord, I worship You...
for speaking so
I can hear Your voice,
For lovingly guiding me
toward the right choice.

Matthew 11:15, Isaiah 58:11

Lord, I worship You...
for leading me to
the Throne of Grace,
For revealing hidden
treasures inside our secret place.

Hebrews 4:16, Daniel 2:19

Lord, I worship You...
for giving me
heavenly wisdom,
For accepting me
into Your kingdom.

Proverbs 2:6, James 1:5, 1 Peter 5:7

Lord, I worship You...
for blessing me
with unmerited favor,
For being my One
and Only Savior.

Proverbs 3:4, Jude 1:25

Lord, I worship You...
for being my
physician and healer,
For being my wise
spiritual leader.

Isaiah 53:5, 1 Timothy 1:17

Lord, I worship You...
for being my deliverer,
For healing me and making
Your plans much clearer.

2 Samuel 22:2, Psalms

Lord, I worship You...
for never leaving
or forsaking me,
For strengthening my heart
as I wait upon Thee.

Hebrews 13:5, Psalm 27:14

Lord, I worship You...
for giving me power
when I feel faint,
For making every
crooked place straight.

Isaiah 40:29, Isaiah 45:2

Lord, I worship You...
for guiding me
into all truth,
For inhabiting my
praises unto You.

John 16:13, Psalm 22:3

Lord, I worship You...
for bringing peace
in every storm,
For performing miracles
each and every morn.

Psalm 107:29, John 3:2

Lord, I worship You...
for carrying my burdens
and sustaining me,
For being in covenant
relationship with me.

Psalm 55:22, Genesis 17:2

Lord, I worship You...
for supping with me
when I open the door,
For lifting my countenance
as I praise You more.

Revelation 3:20, Psalm 42:11

Lord, I worship You...
for putting in my
heart a new song,
For dancing with
me until the dawn.

Ephesians 5:19, Song of Solomon 2:6

Lord, I worship You...
for blessing me with
divine health and rest,
For renewing my strength
so I can give my best.

3 John 2, Isaiah 40:31

Lord, I worship You...
for protecting me
from ungodly wrath,
For being a light
unto my path.

Joshua 9:20, Psalm 119:105

Lord, I worship You...
for communing with me,
For loving me unconditionally.

Psalm 4:4, Romans 8:39

Lord, I worship You...
for answering me
when I call,
For lifting me
whether I fail or fall.

Jeremiah 33:3, Psalm 91:15, Jude 1:24

Lord, I worship You...
for touching me and
turning me around,
For planting my
feet on solid ground.

Jeremiah 10:23, Luke 6:48

Lord, I worship You...
for giving me joy for sorrow,
For giving assurance
for trust in tomorrow.

Proverbs 10:22, Matthew 6:34

Lord, I worship You...
for preserving me with truth,
For living in me to
be salt in the earth.

Psalm 40:11, Matthew 5:13

Lord, I worship You...
for making me
a vessel of love,
For sending the Holy Spirit
from Heaven above.

John 14:26, 15:26

Lord, I worship You...
for keeping my mind
in perfect peace,
For guiding me into
the ways of peace.

Isaiah 26:3, Luke 1:79

Lord, I worship You...
for redeeming what
the enemy's stolen,
For carrying each
and every burden.

Psalm 106:10, 38:4

Lord, I worship You...
for making my
little light shine,
For blessing me
always with a sound mind.

Matthew 5:16, 2 Timothy 1:7

Lord, I worship You...
for making my
way prosperous,
For being my rock
and my fortress.

Joshua 1:8, Psalm 31:3

Lord, I worship You...
for giving me prosperity,
For loosing me from the
spirits of lack and poverty.

Psalm 122:7, Proverbs 11:24, 28:19

Lord, I worship You...
for delivering my
soul from all fear,
For bottling each
and every tear.

Psalm 34:4, 2 Timothy 3:11, Psalm 56:8

Lord, I worship You...
for leading me beside
the still waters,
For expanding my
coast and my borders.

Psalm 23:2, 1 Chronicles 4:10

Lord, I worship You...
for being my
faithful companion,
For teaching me to
be a fisher of men.

Psalm 119:63, Matthew 4:19

Lord, I worship You...
for blessing me
within and without,
For satisfying my
soul in drought.

Proverbs 10:22, Isaiah 58:11

Lord, I worship You...
for making all grace
abound toward me,
For providing Your
grace with sufficiency.

2 Corinthians 9:8, 12:9

Lord, I worship You...
for crowning me
with lovingkindness,
For creating me
in Your likeness.

Psalm 103:4, Genesis 1:27

Lord, I worship You...
for making me a
seed of Abraham,
For giving me truth
upon which I stand.

Psalm 105:6, Galatians 3:16, Ephesians 6:14

Lord, I worship You...
for Your holy presence,
For honoring me as
I give You reverence.

Hebrews 9:24, Psalm 89:7

Lord, I worship You...
for blessing
the work of my hands,
For being with me — wherever
I go, wherever I am!

Deuteronomy 28:2-8, 28:11-12

About the Writer

KATHLEEN SCHUBITZ is an accomplished author, poet, speaker and business woman. God's spoken word from Romans 14:17 birthed RPJ & Company (Righteousness, Peace and Joy) in 2004, thereby establishing a Kingdom publishing business for God's people. As founder and president, her faith in God and desire to follow His leading compels her to pursue her own writing and publish books, devotionals, poetry, calendars, keepsake cards and marketing materials for leaders and Kingdom writers.

After growing up in the Midwestern United States, Kathleen presently resides in central Florida. Preparation for her calling comes from serving at Rotary International headquarters as production assistant for *The Rotarian* magazine. Having now become an inspirational writer, she lives a life of dedication to God, choosing to turn life's hardships into stepping stones for success. Pressing through an oppressive childhood, life-threatening abuse and sickness as an adult, Kathleen allows the Spirit of God to turn her tragedies into triumph and devastation into dedication. Victorious over her own hurtful situations, she now helps others discover truth to live a life of freedom.

A few of Kathleen's published works include the following: *...In His Presence, Scripture Keys, His Heart Calls, Personal Poetic Promises from God's Word* and *ABCs of Who I Am in Christ!* Her prolific skills in writing, proof-editing, design and typography help new and experienced authors publish books and quality products with a spirit of excellence. To learn more about Kathleen Schubitz or publishing and related services by RPJ & Company, visit the website: www.RPJandco.com.

More Books by Kathleen Schubitz

...In His Presence - Color

...In His Presence - B/W

...In His Presence 40-Day Journal

ABCs of Who I Am in Christ!
(for women)

ABCs of Who I Am in Christ!
(for men and women)

ABC Journal to Freedom

ABC Woman Finds Freedom

Finding Purpose after Abuse

His Heart Calls (Devotional)
KJV (Available in Color and B/W)

His Heart Calls (Devotional)
Contemporary (Available in Color and B/W)

Journal to Freedom

Living with Purpose 30-Day Journal

Personal Poetic Promises from God's Word
(Available in Color and B/W)

Scripture Keys

Weekly Planner/Devotional (Any Year)

All books are available through Amazon,
Christian bookstores and at our website:
www.rpjandco.com